Dia~~~~ ~~~ ~ylvia Long

comes this g~~~~~ W~~~~ ~~e fascinating world of nests. From tiny
bee hummin~ ~~~ ~~ests to the towering nests of dusky scrubfowl, an
incredible variety of nests is showcased here in brilliant splendor.
Poetic in voice and elegant in design, this carefully researched book
will spark the imagination of children everywhere.

PRAISE FOR *A NEST IS NOISY*

"Fans will rejoice at the first sight of *A Nest Is Noisy*."
—*School Library Journal*

"This beautiful picture book will be
an asset to science collections." —*Booklist*

"The intricacy and textural variety of nests displays Long's
artistic skill to advantage. . . . Illustrations are a delight
even viewed apart from the text." —*The Bulletin of the
Center for Children's Books*

A Bank Street College of Education
Best Book of the Year

A Junior Library Guild selection

A Parents' Choice Silver Honor

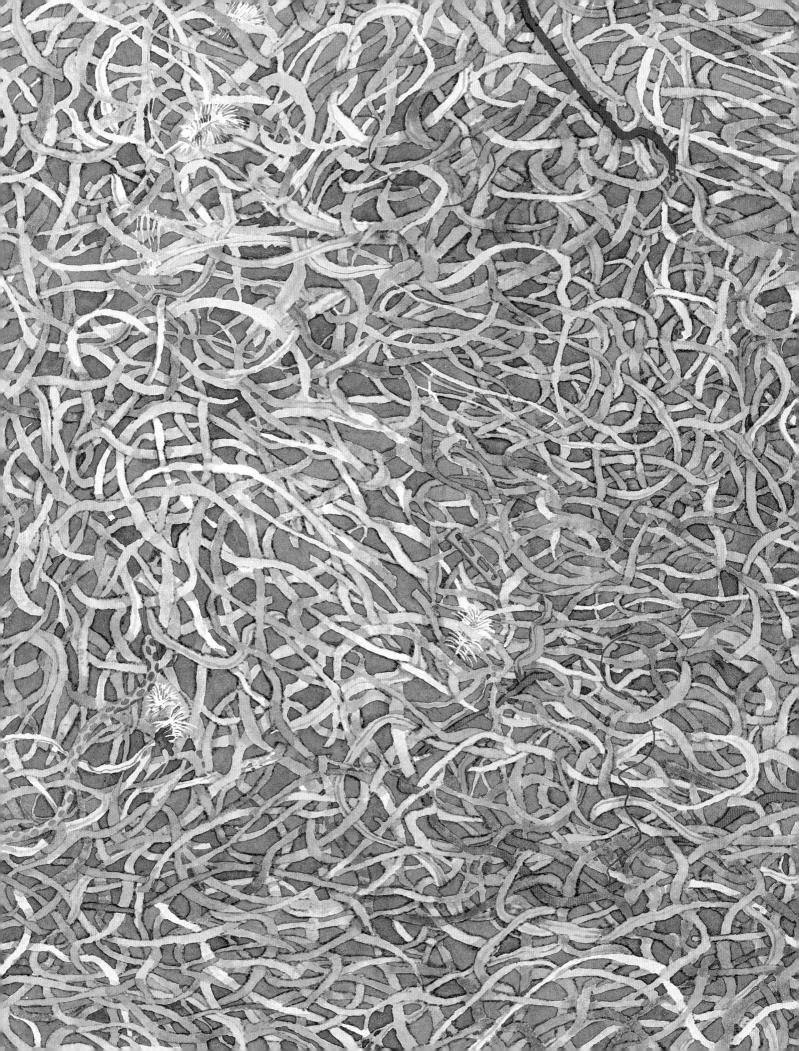

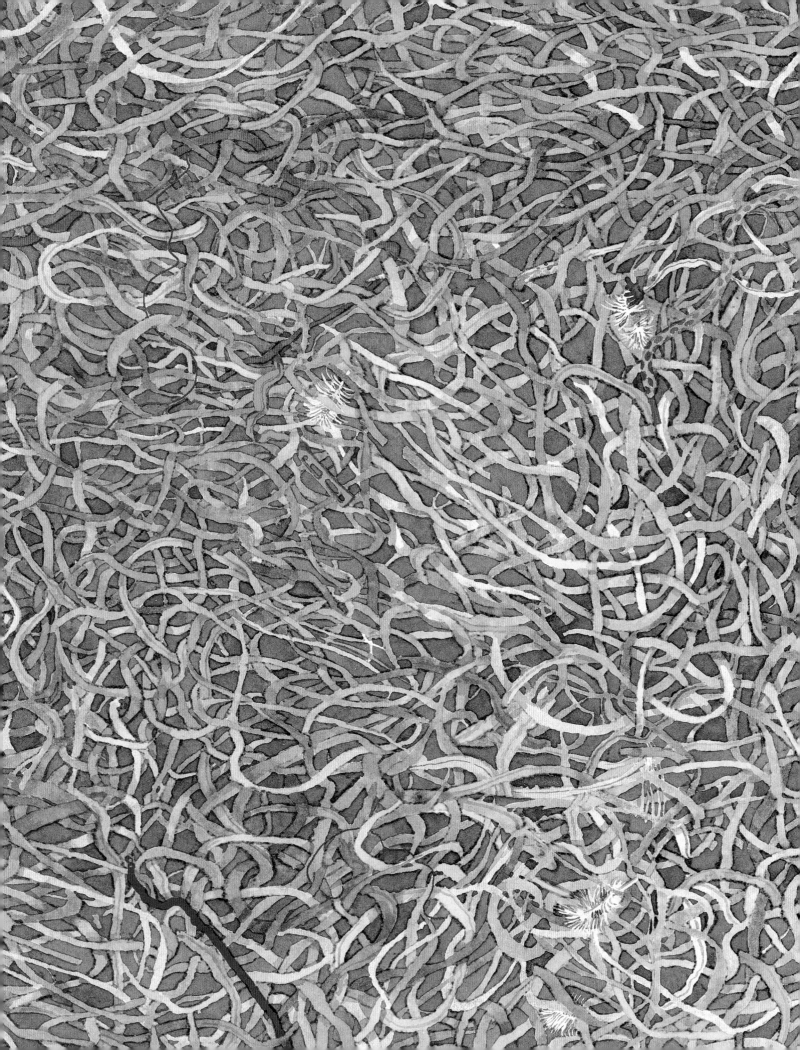

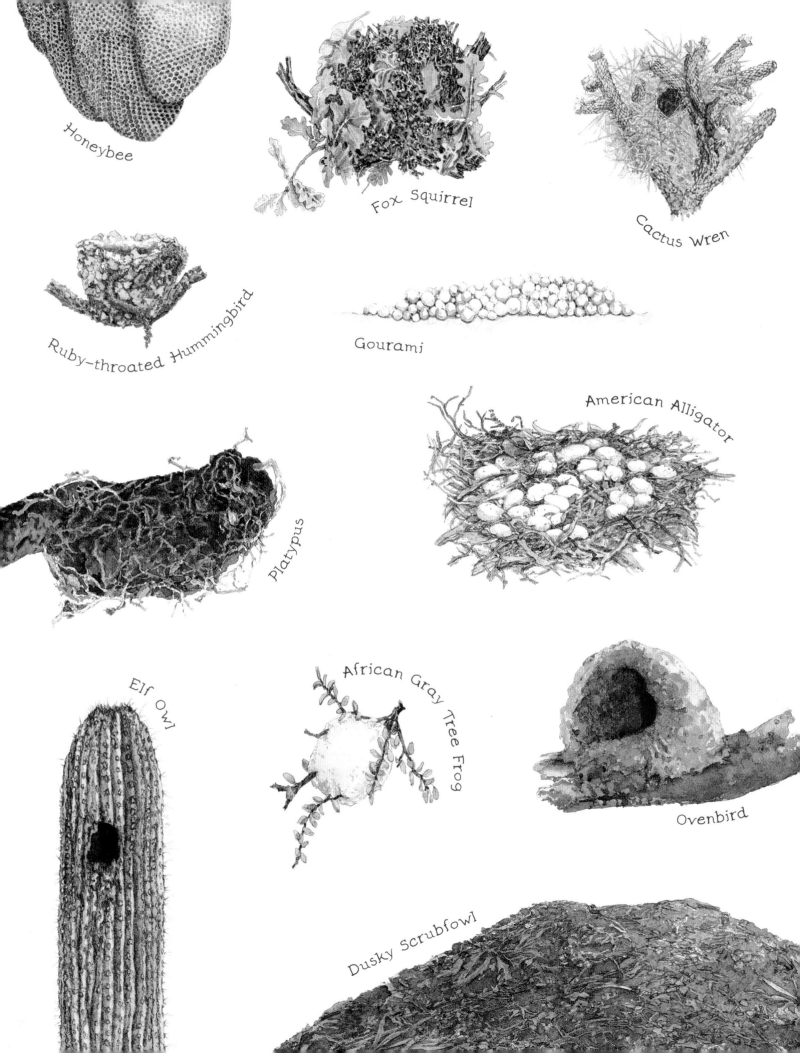

Honeybee

Fox Squirrel

Cactus Wren

Ruby-throated Hummingbird

Gourami

American Alligator

Platypus

Elf Owl

African Gray Tree Frog

Ovenbird

Dusky Scrubfowl

Baya Weaver

Kemp's Ridley Sea Turtle

Bee Hummingbird

Black-tailed Prairie Dog

American Flamingo

Organ-pipe Mud Dauber

Lamprey

Bald-faced Hornet

Blue Jay

Orangutan

Buff-breasted Paradise Kingfisher

Cave Swiftlet

Army Ant

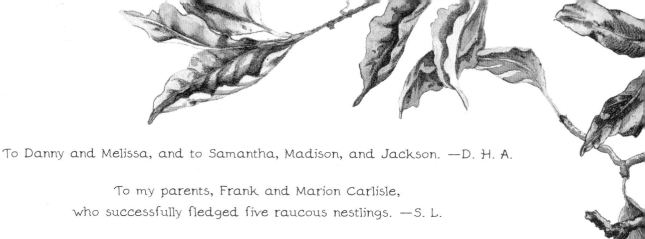

To Danny and Melissa, and to Samantha, Madison, and Jackson. —D. H. A.

To my parents, Frank and Marion Carlisle,
who successfully fledged five raucous nestlings. —S. L.

First Chronicle Books LLC paperback edition, published in 2017.
Originally published in hardcover in 2015 by Chronicle Books LLC.

ISBN 978-1-4521-6135-8

The Library of Congress has cataloged the original edition as follows:
Aston, Dianna Hutts, author.
A nest is noisy / by Dianna Aston ; illustrated by Sylvia Long.
pages cm
Audience: Ages 5–8.
Audience: K to grade 3.
ISBN 978-1-4521-2713-2 (alk. paper)
1. Nests—Juvenile literature. 2. Animals—Habitations—Juvenile literature.
3. Animal behavior—Juvenile literature. I. Long, Sylvia, illustrator. II. Title.

QL676.2.A835 2015
591.56'4—dc23
2013047998

Manufactured in China.

Book design by Sara Gillingham Studio.
Hand lettered by Anne Robin and Sylvia Long.
The illustrations in this book were rendered in watercolor.

10 9 8 7 6 5 4 3

Chronicle Books LLC
680 Second Street
San Francisco, California 94107

Chronicle Books—we see things differently.
Become part of our community at www.chroniclekids.com.

Orangutan

A Nest Is Noisy

Dianna Hutts Aston + Sylvia Long

chronicle books · san francisco

A nest is noisy.

It is a nursery of

chirp-chirping . . .

Ruby-throated Hummingbird

Honeybee

buzzing . . .   squeaking . . .

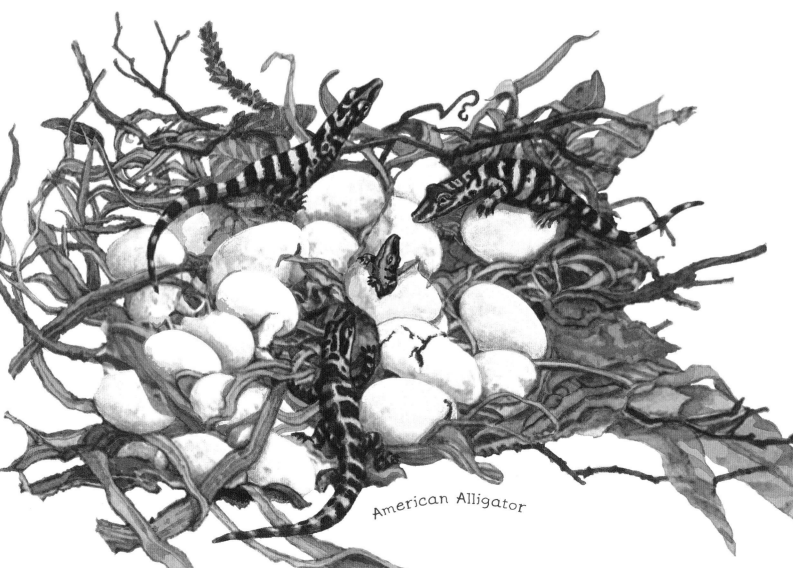

American Alligator

Fox Squirrel

peep-peeping . . .

Gourami

bubbling . . . .

babies.

A nest is welcoming.

Many birds assemble a cradle for their eggs, knitting together leaves and twigs, and softening it with grass, hair, moss, fluffy seeds, leaf skeletons, or even a snake's old skin. They might also add candy wrappers, plastic bags, and bits of cloth or paper.

Blue Jay

Birds are not the only animals that make nests. Orangutans climb high into the rainforest canopy, where each day they braid a new bed of strong branches and line it with a mattress of leaves and twigs. On rainy nights, a woven umbrella of leaves keeps them dry.

A nest is enormous...

One of the largest bird's nests is the dusky scrubfowl's. Their mounded nests are made of decomposing leaves and twigs and can measure more than 36 feet (11 metres) in diameter and nearly 16 feet (5 metres) high.

Dusky Scrubfowl

1' 2' 3' 5' 6' 7' 8' 9' 10' 11' 12' 13' 14' 15' 16' 17'

or tiny.

The smallest bird's nest—the
bee hummingbird's—is a golf ball-size
cup of moss, lichen, bark, and leaves,
usually wrapped in spider's silk.
The stretchy silk lets the nest expand
as the babies grow larger.

Bee Hummingbird

1"   2"   3"   4"

20'   21'   22'   23'   24'   25'   26'   27'   28'   29'   30'   31'   32'   33'   34'   35'

A nest is spiky...

Elf owls and cactus wrens
select a prickly nesting place as
a refuge from slithering snakes
and other hungry hunters.

Elf Owl

Cactus Wren

Bald-faced Hornet

papery . . .

Hornets, yellow jackets, and paper wasps scrape fibers from weathered wood and chew it until it's a moist paste that dries into a tough, paper-like material. The bald-faced hornet queen makes a cell for each egg.

pebbly . . .

Eel-like lampreys use their suction-cup mouths to move stones the size of peas, walnuts, and even base-balls, and create depressions, called *redds*, in shallow streambeds. They lay their eggs in the redds, and cover them with more pebbles to hide them.

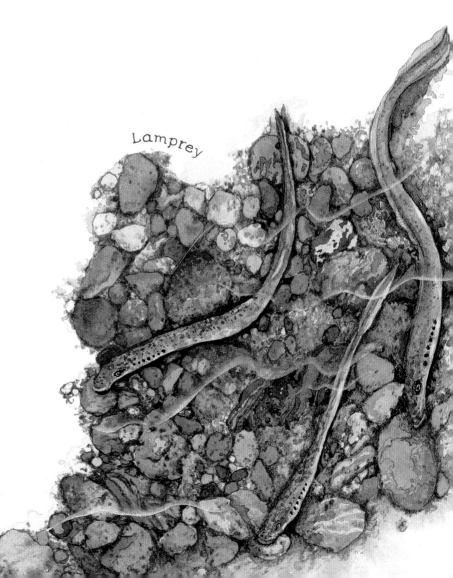

Lamprey

African Gray Tree Frog

African gray tree frogs make a foamy nest
for their eggs in branches overhanging water. With
her hind legs, the female churns a substance
secreted from her body into a frothy mass that,
in sunlight, hardens into a meringue-like crust.
A few days after the tadpoles hatch, the nest
disintegrates and the tadpoles drop into the water
where they can feed and develop into frogs.

bubbly!

Gourami

Gourami blow bubbles that pack
together to form a nest that floats like
a raft in still water. Under the bubble nest,
the male and female *spawn*—produce eggs.
Once the female has released her eggs,
she swims away while the male carries the
eggs in his mouth and places them in the
nest. After they hatch, the baby fish, or
fry, swim beneath the gooey nests, where
they are guarded by the male until they
are ready to strike out on their own.

Ovenbird

Some South American ovenbirds forge an adobe "oven" made with thousands of mud and clay pellets. Baked in the sun, the nest is a cozy place for their eggs.

A nest

An alligator piles decaying plants and
mud to create a mat. In the center she digs
a hole, where she lays her eggs and then, with
her forelimbs and jaws, covers the nest with
more vegetation to keep them warm until they
hatch as squeaking babies. The temperature of
the nest determines the sex of alligators.

is hot.

American Alligator

Kemp's Ridley Sea Turtle

A nest is hidden.

In spring and summer, tens of thousands of female Kemp's ridley sea turtles ride the waves together onto Gulf Coast beaches and drag themselves up to the dunes. They use their hind flippers like shovels to dig a pit in the sand. After the turtle deposits her round, leathery eggs, she tamps down the sand with the underside of her shell and flings more sand over the nest to hide any signs of it.

The platypus—one of only two mammals to lay eggs—hollows out tunnels or burrows along streambeds. With her tail, the female carries moist plant matter deep into the tunnel to make a nest and lays soft-shelled eggs the size of marbles. She adds plugs of soil in the tunnel to protect the eggs from rising waters, predators, and changing temperatures.

Platypus

A nest is neighborly.

There is safety in numbers. Some nest-builders
live in colonies, where there are more ears and
eyes to raise an alarm when *predators*—animals
that eat other animals—are near.

Baya weavers build nests that hang from thorny trees or palm fronds like upside-down bottles. Swinging in the air from a woven tube, each nest is protected from lizards, snakes, and bigger birds.

In "towns" of hundreds of inhabitants, black-tailed prairie dogs make grass-lined nesting chambers within the labyrinth of burrows. When a predator is spotted, the prairie dogs bark to warn their neighbors that danger is near.

Baya Weaver

Black-tailed Prairie Dog

Army ants make "living nests" called *bivouacs*. Clinging to one another's legs and jaws, or *mandibles*, they form a writhing ball of millions of ants, suspended from a branch by a chain of more ants. Inside are chambers for the queen, a brood of eggs, newly hatched larvae, and food.

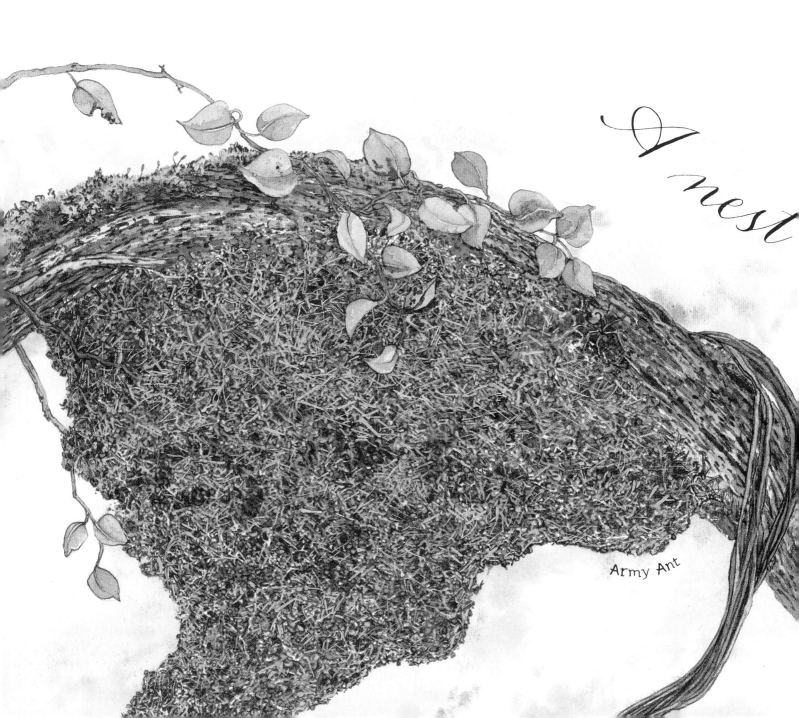

A nest

Army Ant

Cave Swiftlet

...is peculiar.

Cave swiftlets concoct a nest made
entirely of saliva. Swinging its head from side
to side, the male spits long, pearly strands
onto the wall of a cave that harden into a lacy
bowl when exposed to air. Bird's nest soup,
made from swiftlet nests, is among the most
expensive foods eaten by humans.

A nest

is muddy.

Flamingos erect a heap of mud, grass, and stones up to 12 inches (30.5 centimetres) tall and then lay a single egg in a depression at the top. The height protects the egg from changing water levels and excessive ground heat. Both parents feed their hatchlings "crop milk" from their digestive tracts until they leave the nest.

American Flamingo

A nest is adopted.

Some creatures choose nests made
by others to brood their offspring.
Cowbirds and common cuckoos lay their
eggs in nests of other birds, where
they are hatched and raised by the
mother of a different species.

The buff-breasted paradise kingfisher
flies like a torpedo at a termite
nest, smashing into the hard mound with
its beak (and sometimes dying on
impact!) to blast a hole into the side.
Inside the mound, they peck out a
tunnel leading to a chamber, where they
lay their eggs. Termites seal off the
tunnel from the inside, so that their
nests are separate.

Buff-breasted Paradise Kingfisher

Organ-pipe Mud Dauber

A nest is noisy...

Buzzing,
swishing,
rustling,
flapping,
and humming
with babies...

American Flamingo

Kemp's Ridley Sea Turtle

Black-tailed Prairie Dog

but only until they are ready
to fly, swim, or crawl away.

Then a nest is . . .

quiet.

Ruby-throated Hummingbird

Platypus

Blue Jay

Dusky Scrubfowl

Army Ant

Baya Weaver

Buff-breasted Paradise Kingfisher

Kemp's Ridley Sea Turtle

Gourami

Fox Squirrel

American Alligator

Bald-faced Hornet

Elf Owl

African Gray Tree Frog

Ovenbird

Cave Swiftlet

Black-tailed Prairie Dog

Honeybee

Bee Hummingbird

Cactus Wren

Orangutan

American Flamingo

Organ-pipe Mud Dauber

Lamprey

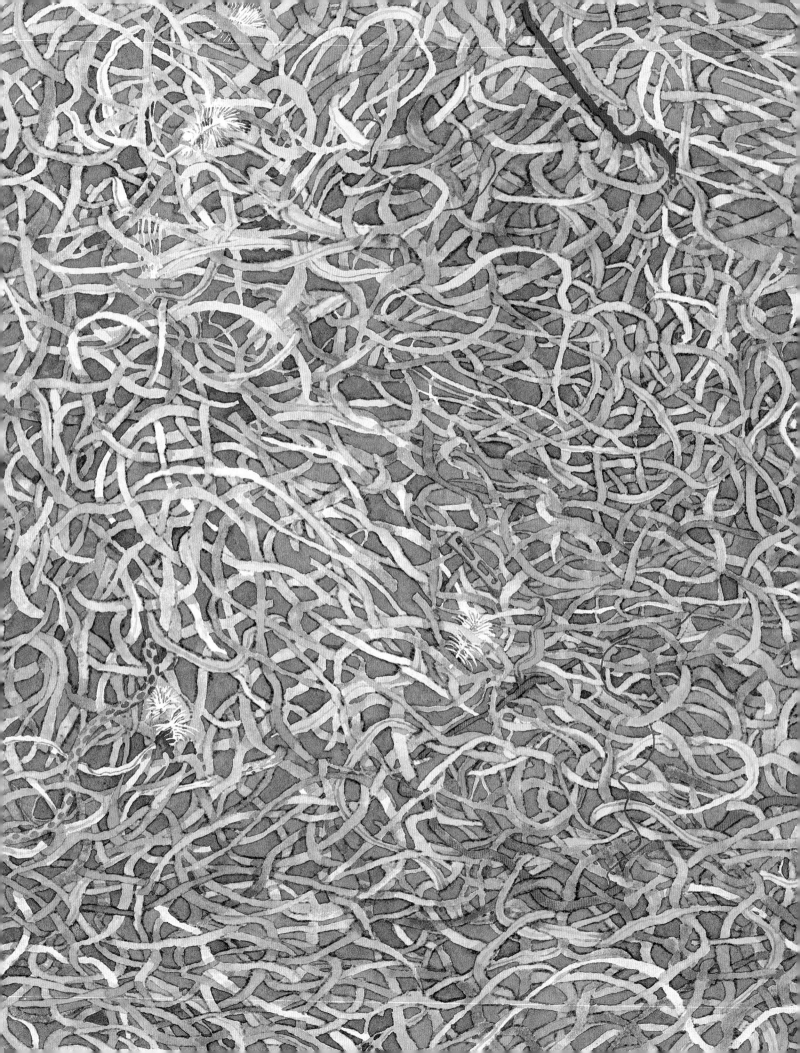

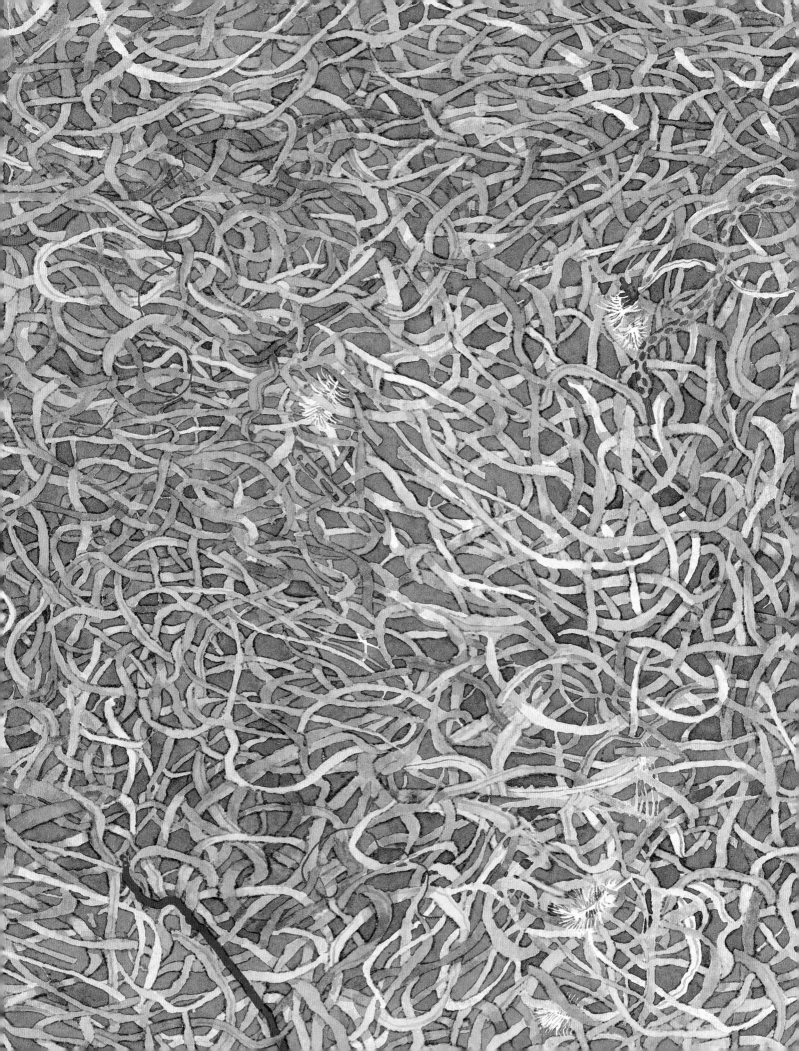

DIANNA HUTTS ASTON is the author of many bestselling books for children and is the founder of SOS: Messages of Love, Hope and Peace. She lives on an island off the coast of Texas. Visit her at www.diannahaston.com.

SYLVIA LONG is the illustrator of many bestselling books for children. Her detailed paintings are inspired by her lifelong interest in nature and its preservation. She lives in Scottsdale, Arizona, with her husband and their dogs. Visit her at www.sylvia-long.com.

ALSO BY DIANNA HUTTS ASTON AND SYLVIA LONG:

A Seed Is Sleepy

★ "Will stretch children's minds and imaginations." —*School Library Journal*, starred review

An IRA Teachers' Choices Reading List selection

An Egg Is Quiet

★ "A delight for budding naturalists of all stripes, flecks, dots, and textures."
—*Kirkus Reviews*, starred review

★ "This attractive volume pleases on both an aesthetic and intellectual level."
—*Publishers Weekly*, starred review

A Junior Library Guild Premiere selection
Scholastic *Parent & Child* Magazine's 100 Greatest Books for Kids
An AAAS/Subaru SB&F Prize for Excellence in Science Books Winner

A Butterfly Is Patient

★ "Both eye-catching and informative." —*School Library Journal*, starred review

★ "A lovely mix of science and wonder." —*Publishers Weekly*, starred review

★ "Stunning." —*Library Media Connection*, starred review

An ALA Notable Children's Book
An NSTA Outstanding Science Trade Book for Students K–12
An NCTE Notable Children's Book in the Language Arts

A Rock Is Lively

"A visual and verbal feast." —*The Boston Globe*

★ "Eye-catching and eye-opening." —*School Library Journal*, starred review

A Boston Globe Best Children's Book of the Year
An IRA Teachers' Choices Reading List selection

A Beetle Is Shy

★ "A sparkling homage to a diverse category of insect." —*Publishers Weekly*, starred review

A Junior Library Guild selection